The Book of Eleven

1.
The Book of Eleven

2.
An itemized collection of brain lint.

3.
19,441 words including "applause," "nothing," "Parmesan," "volume," "stoplight," "I," "subtlety," "in-flight," "fame," "chin," "coffeehouse," and "washcloth."

4.
Cameos by David Eggers, Charise Mericle, and my brother Joe.

5.
A tour-de-force of humanity, culture and olives.

6.
Nonfiction, nonlinear, and nondenominational.

7.
"When Amy is at her best, she is able to see the everyday unseen . . . and describe it with both precision and with great, humane wit. When she's at her worst, she punches people."
—David Eggers, editor-at-large, *Esquire* magazine

8.

A choppy, decentralized memoir.

9.

"Is it the wind in the Windy City . . . that enables Amy Krouse Rosenthal to see the world so clearly? Or maybe it's just lack of sleep. For whatever reason, in The Book of Eleven, *she illuminates the shadowy corners of modern life with the wit and wisdom of a sage— only she'd never admit to knowing a thing."*

—Craig Cox, managing editor, *Utne Reader*

10.

You may be thinking, "Man, I could have written this."

Well, that's probably true.

11.

By Amy Krouse Rosenthal

**Andrews McMeel
Publishing**

Kansas City

www.andrewsmcmeel.com

Design by Blair Graphic Design

98 99 00 01 02 RDC 10 9 8 7 6 5 4 3 2 1

Library of Congress Cataloging-in-Publication Data
Rosenthal, Amy Krouse.
   The book of eleven : an itemized collection of brain lint / by Amy Krouse Rosenthal.
       p. cm.
   The t.p. data are arranged as a list of eleven numbered segments, with the title proper listed under "1," the subtitle under "2," other statements about the book under "3"–"10," and the author statement under "11."
   ISBN 0-8362-6775-3 (hardcover)
1. American wit and humor. I. Title.
PN6162.R6545 1998
811'.5402—dc21

                98-14068
                CIP

For Jason, who, in the summer of '89, wooed me with 11 roses.

Contents

11 acknowledgments

1.

I WANT TO THANK Dr. Seuss and his classic *My Book About Me* for introducing me to the process of putting thoughts down on paper, resulting in self-examination and unwarranted self-importance.

2.

I WANT TO THANK all those who read and improved my manuscript: Jason Rosenthal, Ann and Paul Krouse, Katie and Adam Froelich, Beth "Peka" Kaufmann, Joe(y) Krouse, David T. Jones (who comes up quite a bit in the book—he's funny, really funny), Charise Mericle, Dave Eggers, Jo "Mil" and Todd Lief, Michel Rosenthal, Arnie Rosenthal, and "Sara and Anna's dad."

3.

I WANT TO THANK James "Stump" Mahoney for producing and engineering the original "Eleven" radio recordings, and, in chronological order, the editors who made this book possible: Dan Barron (*Art Direction*), Dave Eggers (*Might*), Stephanie Bennett and Chris Schillig (Andrews McMeel).

4.

I WANT TO THANK my agent whose name I'd rather not say because he's the best agent in the world and then other really *good* writers will track him down and they'll get all chummy together and it will become harder and harder for me to get ahold of him, and, well, we all know how it goes from there.[1]

5.

I WANT TO THANK John Fernandez for setting me up on the blind date of my life.

6.
I want to thank Justin, Miles, and Paris.

7.

I WANT TO THANK my parents for everything they didn't say, didn't do, and pretended not to see while I was growing up.

8.

I WANT TO THANK Chris Fleissner, Santina Gobel, Sara Hernandez, and Ning Gary for their invaluable contributions, support, and overall amazingness; Lisa von Drehle for braining the name "Brain Lint"; and, without going into the details, Alex Chadwick, Art Silverman, and Bob Hawkinson.

9.

I WANT TO THANK Tom Handley and Urbus Orbis coffeehouse for injecting Charise and me with coffee and hope every Thursday for three years, and Emily Oberman and Bonnie Siegler for injecting *The Book of Eleven* with a generous dose of Number Seventeen.

10.

I WANT TO THANK anyone who ever reads this book. Let me know who you are, and I promise to E-mail you back a personal thank-you. Please specify whether or not you like focaccia bread. (amy@suba.com)

11.

I WANT TO THANK my lucky stars.

11 introductions

1.

WHY 11? A LIST OF 9 felt too short. Letterman owns 10©.
And 12 seemed like a lot of work.

2.

While writing this book, I came across a
little bag at Urban Outfitters whose label
read "Eleven Eleven." Always on the hunt for
a good synchronistic omen, I took it as a sign
("Eleven Eleven— Ohmygodthat'ssoweird.")
and bought it, figuring if anything had the
power to help The Book of Eleven find a
publisher, why not a funky, pink bag?[2]

3.

PORTIONS OF THIS BOOK previously appeared in some form in *Might* magazine, *Art Direction*, *Utne Reader*, *New City*, *Parenting*, *Green*, *Chicago Reader*, *Digital City*, and on WBEZ radio. Thank you to David Eggers, Dan Barron, Rebecca Scheib, Frank Sennett, Dale Conour, Ken Kurson, Alison True and Cate Plys, Royce Vibbert and Aaron Freeman, respectively.

4.

PORTIONS OF THIS BOOK previously appeared as cryptic notes scribbled on Post-its, cash machine receipts, and my palm.

5.

IT'S HARD TO WRITE A BOOK, you know? When you begin each week, perched from the vantage point of Monday, you think you will have all this time—large, blank chunks before and after a few obligatory appointments and errands—where you will just sit down, uninterrupted, and write your head off. But invariably, as each day presents itself, as it becomes a true day (as opposed to the surreal, vacant, unscheduled "tomorrow" it was in your mind just yesterday), there are unsatisfying but not unnecessary things that take you away from your computer, such as running out for Scotch tape, renewing your driver's license, getting a mole checked.

6.

WE WERE AT A FRIEND'S for dinner and she said, "So tell me about the book—what's it called again?"

"*The Book of Eleven*," I said.

"What's that? *The Beckoning of Lovely*?"

The Beckoning of Lovely. That sounded great to me, so gloriously obscure and literary. I reluctantly corrected her.

7.

COMPARTMENTALIZING the world into tiny, manageable pieces gives the compartmentalizer an addicting sense of security and power.

8.

THIS BOOK REALLY NEEDS no introduction. So, here it is . . . *The Book of Eleven*.

9.

I FEEL SAFE AND HAPPY around those people who make lists, for I know that if they say they will do something—say, fax me an article or order theater tickets—they will write it down, which is an absolute precursor to actually doing it. Then they will fax me/order the tickets so they can cross it off their list. This is simply the way list-people operate.

10.

WHEN I THINK OF INTRODUCTIONS I can't help but think of my friend—let's call him Paul Safsel of New York—who was being introduced to this woman at a party, and after the Paul-this-is-Megan-Megan-this-is-Paul part, she leaned forward and said, "I'm sorry, I didn't catch your income."

11.

AN INTRODUCTION is the parsley of literature: you don't *really* need it, most people don't even *notice* it, but somehow your concoction seems incomplete without it.

11 thoughts about the movies

1.

PEOPLE OFTEN SAY, "Why would I want to see a depressing movie? When I go to the movies, I want to be *entertained*." But when I see a depressing movie about heroin addicts or rejected fat people or a woman who is being cheated on while dying of some rare disease in a hospital, that's when I leave feeling happy and grateful for my life. However, when I see a movie where some beautiful actress with a flat stomach meets a rich man with a flat stomach and they constantly achieve mutual orgasm in his five-thousand-square-foot loft, *that's* when I get depressed.

2.

OFTEN, WHEN SOMEONE says something funny, my immediate reaction is: "What's that from again?" It's like if I can't place the line from a popular movie, it wouldn't necessarily occur to me that it was simply an original thought.

3.

While I love watching all the previews at the movies, they also make me very anxious. I can feel myself frantically making a mental list of all the ones I have to see and when. It gets to the point where I am actually <u>relieved</u> when a preview looks really bad, so at least that's one less movie I have to remember to see.

4.

I ALWAYS WANT TO SEE what happens after the movie's technically "over." I want an update on the couple that fell in love in Dolby Surround Sound, to see how they're doing post-euphoria. Have they begun fighting over small increments of time? (*"You said you'd be home at 7:15. It's 7:20."*) Or like in *Ransom*, after they get their son back in the end, I wanted to see what their family life was like. When they're sitting around the breakfast table, do they reminisce, "Can you *believe* you were chained up to a bed for a week?"

5.

Musicals have always made me uncomfortable and wince-y. The way two people will be having a nice chat and then suddenly, inexplicably, one of them bursts into song and the other one has to join in. I actually feel embarrassed for the actors, because you know that they too would be much more comfortable just speaking at a moment like that.

6.

NOTHING MAKES me feel more alienated, more uninvited, more removed from the impenetrable clique-of-cool, than hearing a celebrity on *Letterman* refer to Robert DeNiro as *Bobby*.

7.

MY PARENTS WERE at the movies and about midway through the film, the fire alarm went off. They were all instructed to vacate the theater for about ten minutes, and when they were allowed back in, everyone went back to their exact same seats.

8.

SIMPLY BASED on a poster that contains a few glib words like, "She found love, then lost herself . . ." next to a gorgeous, retouched photograph of two actors I happen to like, I'll think, "Wow. That movie looks *really* good." Intellectually, I know how contrived and strategic and misleading and Hollywood-ized the poster really is, but still, I fall for it every time.

9.

WHEN A GOOD FRIEND TOLD ME she actually walked out of one of my all-time favorite movies,[3] our entire friendship flashed before me: could all my perceptions about her be wrong? Maybe she isn't the cool, intelligent person I thought she was. In that one irrational moment, every positive trait she possessed was canceled out by the fact that she didn't like this movie, that she wasn't exactly like me.

10.

YOU KNOW HOW YOU'LL be watching a movie where the main characters are in a public place, usually a restaurant, and so there are all these other people—extras—sitting around their tables talking? What do the extras talk about? Does the director tell them to engage in "real" conversation, or just do fake mumbly stuff? I try to watch their mouths closely, but it's hard to tell. Anyway, either way, don't they feel really awkward and self-conscious?

11.

IF MY FRIEND PAT doesn't like a movie, he has to immediately go see another one because he can't stand the thought of having the last movie he saw be that bad one. He says, "What if I get hit by a truck? I'll be lying there dying thinking, 'I can't believe that was the last movie I'll ever see.'"

11 thoughts about planes and flying

1.

EVERY TIME I'M FLYING and the captain announces we're beginning our descent, the same thing goes through my mind. While we're still pretty high above the city, I'll think, if the plane went down now, we would definitely not be OK. A bit lower, and no, we still wouldn't be OK. But as we get real close to the ground, I'll think, OK, we're low enough, if it crashed now, we might be OK.

2.

MY HUSBAND AND I were at the airport. While he was across the way getting coffee and I was waiting reading the paper, he mouthed something to me. I thought he was trying to tell me that a famous person was right there, check it out! So I'm frantically searching, but couldn't find anyone. I looked back at him with squinty eyebrows and upturned palms, and mouthed, "Where?!" fearing The Famous Person was already too far away to be spotted. I then realized he was simply saying, "Bring me the sports section."

3.

PEOPLE ARE either good or bad at their profession—good and bad accountants, good and bad artists. What then constitutes a bad air traffic controller, and what needs to happen before he/she is fired?

4.

If a plane of lobsters went down in the Andes mountains and they had to canni-balize one another, they'd be psyched. "Lobster again? Excellent!"

5.

AS I WALK THROUGH first class to get to my coach seat, I always quickly eye the first-class delegates, trying to figure out what they do or who they "are" that enables them to fly so elitely. I'm always extra-intrigued by those unassuming types: a disheveled teenager; an un-rich–looking fat guy; an old lady. It would be so helpful for us coach travelers to be given a First-Class Roster, disclosing the gossipy details of their good fortune.

SEAT 2A: Trust-fund kid. Flying to his moth-er's wedding (third marriage).

SEAT 3C: 3C's great-grandfather made a fortune when he invented the washcloth.

SEAT 5B: Racked up enough miles to upgrade.

6.

AFTER WATCHING a news report of a small plane that went down "killing two," my reaction, much to my horror and shame, was actually disappointment. I thought, "Only two? That's nothing," and I changed the channel.

7.

I WAS SITTING NEXT to this engineer-type on an airplane and was suddenly drawn to the big, Xeroxed document he was reading. It was titled, "Surface Micromachines Gyroscope Fabrication." That's the *exact* title; I was so intrigued by the words that I surreptitiously copied them down word for word. About an hour later we started chatting and he told me he worked for the government. I said, "What do you do?" And he said, "I can't tell you. It's classified."

8.

WHEN YOU FLY you get to see all kinds of people—conservative businessmen being especially rewarding—sleep with their mouths hanging open.

ONE TIME I WAS ALMOST at the airport before I realized I left my wallet at home. I was flying to New York, the city least likely to be kind and understanding to a wallet-less soul. But I really needed to get on that flight to make a meeting a couple hours later, so I decided to board and pray for the best, nervously confident that I would figure *something* out. The first part of the flight I just cried, wallowing in my stupidity. The second part of the flight I panicked. And about ten minutes before landing I extracted all the courage in my body to ask the woman next to me if I could borrow some money just to get me to my hotel, "and I'll mail you a check, I swear." After babbling my saga of woe and spaciness to her, one question led to another, and it turned out I knew her son, who lived and worked in New York. The satisfying epilogue was that a couple weeks later, when I was back in Chicago, I got a call from her: "I received this check from you, and I don't know who you are or why you gave it to me." I had to actually *remind* her of the whole episode, which I could not believe, and which just about matched me in absentmindedness.

10.

CONSIDERING HOW MUCH they're advertised in the in-flight magazines, it looks like someone is actually buying those "YOUR LOGO HERE" watches.

11.

I CAN'T HELP MYSELF from saving leftover food from my in-flight meal—a pack of Sun Chips, a prepackaged oatmeal raisin cookie, a banana—and hoarding it in my purse for that moment later when I will be absolutely famished and miles from civilization. Then I end up shuttling it back and forth between purse/backpack/suitcase, schlepping it home, then finally throwing it out a couple weeks later.

ll rules of humanity

1.

IF SOMEONE STARTS a sentence with "I love him to death" or "I love him like a brother" or "Don't get me wrong," guaranteed, a nasty insult will follow. (*"I love him like a brother, but he's a selfish bastard."*)

2.

IF SOMEONE WHO JUST met a famous person says, "Oh, they were really nice, really down to earth," this basically means the famous person paid attention to the non-famous person for a millisecond or two. But if they say, "Oh, he was a jerk, really cocky," it just means that the non-famous person went completely unnoticed by the famous person.[4]

3.

WHEN SOMEONE IS INJURED or has to have some growth removed, it is invariably "1 millimeter away" from something much more serious and/or fatal. "If the fracture was one millimeter to the left, I'd be paralyzed/blind/dead."

Cameo!!! Please welcome David Eggers . . .[5]

4.

NON PROFIT DIRECT MAIL Solicitations ARE ALMOST invARiably PAiRED with CUSTOMiZED RETURN-ADDRESS labels. "FREE GiFT ENCLOSED!" the envelopES SHRiEK, AND iNSiDE, BESiDES A PLEA foR CASH FROM GREENPEACE oR JiMMY + ROSALYNN CARTER, You Get A hUNDRED oR So StickERS with YOUR NAME MiSSPELLED ON THEM. It's LiKE A RULE oF the tRADE; You SiMPLY DON'T FiND A SOLiCitAtiON WithOUt the Little LABELS, AND you CERtAiNLY NEvER FiND THE LABELS — the KiND with the SCREENED-BACK iMAGE OF A BALD EAGLE OR the StAtUE OF LiBERtY— OUtSiDE thESE SOLiCitAtiONS. IF you KNOW WHERE the PRACtiCE ORiGiNAtED, OR to WHOM WE COULD SEND THANKS, PLEASE CALL ME iN the EVENiNG At HOME: 212·666-1815.

5.

IF YOU BUY GREENISH BANANAS at the grocery store
so they will last a few days at home, when you actually remember they are there and/or you're in the mood for one, they will
be brown.

6.

If you make eye contact with someone who's
trying to catch the elevator, you are
obligated to hold the door for them. If
no eye contact is made, it is customary
to act like you are reaching for the
"door open" button and then let it close
in their face.

7.

THE UNFLATTERING THING about yourself that you are sure everyone thinks about day and night, and relentlessly snickers about in your absence, I promise, if you bring it up, no one will even know what you're talking about. (Like when I hadn't seen Uncle B. for a couple years and the first thing he said to me was: "I want to apologize for eating all your pâté last time I saw you.")

8.

THE FLATTERING THING you imagine everyone's thinking about you isn't at all. (Like when D. thought everyone was staring at him because he looked especially fabulous that day, but it turned out he just had cream cheese on his chin.)

9.

IF YOU LISTEN to a favorite mixed-tape for weeks and come to know not just the order of the songs but the exact pausing in between, when you happen to hear one of those songs on their original album, it will really throw you.

10.

IF YOU'RE HANGING OUT with someone, and they wipe their nose, you think it's a signal that you've got a booger. So you wipe your nose, but then they think you're signaling them. And this goes on and on, with the only real resolution being that both parties accept the fact that they may have a booger.

11.

Not before, not after. But _during_ college, you will think milk crates make super bookshelves.

11 quick calculations

1.

Depression + Hair Spray = Country Music

2.

Relatives + Turkey = Depression

3.

99 Bottles of Beer on the Wall - 99 Luft Balloons = Zero Mostel

4.

Money + Ignorance = Television

5.

(Patience + Insight) x Coffee = Poetry

6.

(Patience + Silence) x Beer = Fishing

7.

Sundays + Chinese Food = Reformed Judaism

8.

(Wonderment + Macaroni 'n' Cheese) - Driver's License = Childhood

9.

(Rented Movie + Couch) +/- 30 minutes = Sleep

10.

(Rice Krispie Treats + Free Sex) - Consequence = Utopia

11.

Lukewarm Coffee x (Telemarketers + Bennigan's) = Hell

ll really short, really true stories

l.

I was getting a massage and the masseuse starts talking to me about dogs, and how great it is to have a pet. I tell her I'm not really a pet person, but she's convinced I'd be happier with one. She says, "You know, you should get a poodle. They're the perfect pet— they don't shit." I say, "That's really weird. I've never heard of such a thing." She's like, "Yeah, isn't that great?!" I'm very confused by this notion, but then I start to drift off. About twenty minutes later, I startle myself awake. "Shed." She said, "Poodles don't SHED."

2.

WE WERE HAVING one of those closet organizing companies redo a couple bedroom closets. On the morning they were supposed to do the work, we received a panicky call from the owner saying they had an unexpected closet emergency with another customer, and they'd have to reschedule. I hung up wondering, what—and I really truly am curious—what exactly constitutes a "closet emergency"?

3.

THE OTHER DAY AT WORK, my friend David threw a crumpled-up piece of paper to me. I caught it, looked at it, then set it down. He then threw a paper clip. I did the same thing. "Don't you get it?!" He yelled. "You're supposed to throw it back!" How was I supposed to know that was what he wanted? I am a girl. I do not have the catch gene. Guys have the catch gene. That is why—and I only realize this now—that the male symbol is ♂. It stands for "throw the ball." ✍

When my fiancé and I
got engaged
he decided to sell his
VW Rabbit because
we only needed one car
and his was a stick
which I didn't know how to drive.
He put an ad in the
local paper that read,
"Must sell car -
fiancée can't drive stick."
We came home one night
to this message
on his machine:
"Yo, dickhead -
teach the bitch
to
drive stick!"

5.

WHILE WALKING TO work and frantically going over the day's upcoming events, I suddenly thought about something I had read the night before—that cliché about really trying to live in the moment. So I shut my thoughts off and started to hear birds chirping. I realized I had never heard these birds before, despite the fact that I walked the same path many times. For the rest of my walk, I listened to and thought about the birds—wondering if they were cold, where they were headed, and so on. Later that afternoon, I was reviewing a designer's portfolio. He showed me a poster he was particularly fond of. In big, bold letters across the top it said: **LISTEN FOR THE BIRDS**.

6.

MY FRIEND DAVID peed right next to Stevie Wonder once.

7.

MY BROTHER-IN-LAW Adam was over and we were all hanging out watching the basketball game. Upset by a play, oblivious to the toddler in our midst, and in full testosterone form, Adam screamed to the TV, "WHAT ARE YOU THINKING? YOU GODDAMN STUPID MOTHERFUCKER!!!" Without missing a beat, three-and-a-half-year-old Justin blurted out, "Uncle Adam, we don't say 'stupid'!"

8.

AFTER COMPLAINING TO my friend Charise about how most guys are so unchatty, she shared with me the dating wisdom of her bisexual friend. Apparently this woman had just come out of a relationship with a real taciturn guy, and then started seeing another woman who turned out to be quite a talker. It was a thrill at first—all the long, animated conversations. No more "Nothing" replies to the question "What are you thinking about?" But then, after some time, she said she was just so damn sick of all the talking. And she made the lane change back to guys.

9.

I OBSERVED this flashing message—which is basically the story of Western Civilization in twenty words or less—on one of those electronic billboards outside a local drugstore:

ONE HOUR PHOTO FINISHING!
CASH STATION INSIDE!
CHICAGO T-SHIRTS!
HIV-TESTS, $39.99!
MUPPET VIDEO!

10.

MY FRIEND PAT WAS BUYING HIS daily paper from a newspaper box. As he straightened himself out and turned to walk away, he realized that his tie had gotten closed in the box. He then also realized that he had no more change. After craning his neck for a moment or two—in search of a kind stranger, or for some answer in general—he did the only sensible thing. He undid his tie, left it in the box, and walked away.

11.

I'M IN THE EMERGENCY room waiting to be examined (for some chest pains, turned out to be nothing), when who appears before me but a guy I went to grammar school with. I can't believe it—the doctor is Jonathan Handler. We both freak out, oh, my God, is it really you, oh, my God. He examines me, we talk, and he goes to call my OB-GYN (I'm pregnant at the time and she needs to check things out, too). She shows up and says before I can have the necessary lung tests, I need to have a rectal exam (I don't understand the correlation either), done typically by the ER doctor. I panic. No way. No way is Jonathan Handler giving me a rectal. "We were in the same third-grade class," I whine. And you know, if you were in the same third-grade class with someone, they can't give you a rectal, that's just the rule. She completely understands and generously offers to do the honors herself. I'm immensely grateful. A few minutes later, Jonathan reappears. He looks nervous. Fidgeting with his hands and avoiding eye contact, he starts to mumble something about necessary procedure, has to be done . . . and I realize he doesn't know the rectal thing's all taken care of. "It's OK!!!" I reassure him. "She already did it!" Jittery awkwardness is replaced with a smirky-smile of relief. He confides that he too was panic-stricken, pleading with his fellow doctors to do him this one favor, that he just couldn't bring himself to do a rectal exam on Amy Krouse.

11 things I'm not proud of but would admit for a small amount of money

1.

I GET A WEEKLY MASSAGE, and try to think about profound things, but mostly just end up with thoughts like, "How many sheets would have to be piled on top of me right now to crush me to death?"

2.

I recently had a very pleasant, erotic dream about Rush Limbaugh. (Yes, _of course_ I find him utterly repulsive in my waking state.)

3.

I WAS OLDER THAN I SHOULD HAVE BEEN when I realized that the word "Colonel" was pronounced "kernel."

4.

I AM A GLUTTON FOR praise, a sucker for compliments. They need not be sincere, or come from someone whose opinion I respect. If someone who I think has consistently bad taste (i.e., likes things I despise and vice versa) pays me a compliment, I'll think, "Oh, this is the *one* time they actually know what they're talking about."

Conversely, if it's a person who flatters merely as a cheap conversational accessory ("Hi-how-are-you-you-look-great"), I'll likewise think, "This is the one time they really mean it." In short, I am an Applause Junkie.

5.

IN JUNIOR HIGH, I went to a Neil Diamond concert with my entire family.

6.

Often, I'll be in the bathroom at work and realize I put my underpants on inside out.

7.

WHEN SOMEONE TELLS ME something really tragic and horrible, I have this nervous habit of smirking.

8.

WHEN SOMEONE MAKES a big mistake, I want them not only to admit their incompetence, their stupidity, their *complete* ignorance, but to scream to the world "I am a loser!" and to announce that having made such a blatant, unforgivable mistake, they have no choice but to quit their job and leave town, which would be the only way to *truly* eliminate the possibility of screwing up and inconveniencing me again, and then, knowing that they deserve everything that's coming to them, they slowly spiral down into oblivion.

9.

I CAN'T NOT LAUGH when someone says the word "duty."

10.

I STILL FIND IT AMUSING when I see a person's tooth colored in black in a photograph.

11.

UP UNTIL about sophomore year of college, I was really into *Ziggy*.

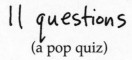
11 questions
(a pop quiz)

1.

WHEN THE WAITER COMES to take your order, do you open your menu again even though you know exactly what you're having?

2.

HOW MANY HOURS can you go reheating the same cup of coffee in the microwave?

3.

DO YOU ALWAYS CHECK for names you know in the Letters to the Editor section of magazines and newspapers, and in those mailing list registration books at stores?

4.

WHEN YOU GET A GOOD letter in the mail, can you wait to read it later when you have more time, or do you have to tear it open right away and read it on the spot?

5.

DO YOU PUT food down the disposal or scrape it into the garbage?

6.

CAN YOU BE A FEMINIST yet still do a double take when you see a woman UPS driver?

7.

WHEN YOU ROAST a marshmallow, do you like to slowly golden-brown it, or catch it on fire for that quick, crispy burn taste?

8.

WHY DO BIRDS suddenly appear every time you are near?

9.

DO YOU REMEMBER learning in grade school that if you typed 7734 on a digital calculator and then turned it upside-down, it would read "hELL?"

10.

DO YOU FEEL LIKE you're doing something wrong when you have to use Kleenex as toilet paper or toilet paper as Kleenex?

11.

WHAT WOULD YOU hang over your bed in jail?

BONUS QUESTION:

I ONCE PICKED LORETTA Swit up at the airport. True or False?

11 cases of feeling torn

1.

A VERY DARK-SKINNED black gentleman was waiting on me at the coffeehouse and I asked for some coffee and a chocolate-covered graham cracker. The very dark-skinned black gentleman asked if I preferred light or dark (chocolate) and I replied, "Light," and there was a split second there where I felt like I could have possibly said the wrong thing.

2.

WE'VE GOT a tri-compartmentalized recycle bin in our kitchen: paper, plastic, and everyday trash. There are a number of items that repeatedly baffle me. Like the frozen juice containers: the cardboard cylinder belongs in paper but the bottom is metal. I'll go back and forth on this for a while, then typically settle on "everyday" instead.

3.

I FOUND A CRINKLED-UP piece of paper on the ground next to my car. It had the addresses and phone numbers to various apartments around town, with several crossed off. I realized it was someone's apartment-hunting list. I didn't know whether to put it back on the ground (littering?) in the outside chance the person would retrace his/her steps looking for it. Or to take it with me to throw out (stealing?).[6]

4.

OUR NEIGHBOR, who's ten, was ranting about a counselor at her sleep-away camp who told everyone he was a vegetarian, but then on the last day of camp when the parents came and brought great food for a big all-camp picnic, this counselor caved and took *three* pieces of Kentucky Fried Chicken (against camp rules: one per person). Her disgust and disbelief epitomized the schism between her world and ours: hers was still one of gray-free absolutes. You're either a kid or a grown-up; a good guy or a bad guy; a chicken-eater or not a chicken-eater.

5.

I was writing at a coffeehouse and this guy starts talking to me, how's it going, what do you do, etc. I'm not overly chatty, not wanting to lead him on, yet as I'm leaving, he asks me if I ever want to go out.* I tell him thanks, but I'm married, kids, whole bit. It then somehow comes up that he works for the local paper. <u>Shit</u>. I could really use a good contact there, but flirting at this point — and I play the whole thing back in my mind in 1.5 seconds — no, retro-flirting is completely out of the question.

* I was breast-feeding at the time and my boobs were <u>huge</u>.

6.

IT WAS SO MUCH EASIER to get out of certain obligations when you were a kid. If you didn't feel quite up for gym class, Mom would just write a note. There are many social situations where I'm wavering (*I should go. But I'm not in the mood. But I should really go.*) and would love to have my mom work her cursive magic.

Please excuse Amy from tonight's dinner party. She is not feeling up to making small talk, looking for a parking spot or putting on matching clothes.

Thank you for your understanding,
Mrs. Krouse

7.

A rainy day can really come as a relief;
it feels cozy and secure because it legit-
imizes — or rather, _forces_ — you to stay
safely inside. But then if the sun comes
out in the afternoon, I'll feel disappointed,
or even scared, because I know the
world will now resume. People will get
dressed and leave their houses and go
places and do things. I'll feel _over-_
whelmed, mentally unprepared to venture
out into the big, busy, sunny world that
was so quiet and soft just a few minutes
ago.

8.

SOME NIGHTS I think, tonight I'm going to stay up all night and create. I'm going to stay up all night and drink lots of coffee and get wired and just writeandthinkandfuckingcreatethehelloutofthenight like no one ever has before. I'm going to stay up even after the damn TV goes to sleep. I'm going to stay up and start a revolution. I'm going to stay up while the rest of the lazy world sleeps and how could *anyone* sleep, there's just so much thinking that needs to be done. I'm going to stay up, I'm really going to do it, I'm going to face the night, I'm going to change the world. But then it gets late and I get tired and I go to sleep.

9.

I CAN'T DECIDE IF I WANT TO PUT THIS ONE IN . . .

10.

I HAD GIVEN MY SON a hard-boiled egg to eat while I was driving him to school, and after taking one bite, he handed it to me: "Here, Mom—I'm done." I didn't want it either but now here I was, driving with one hand, and holding this slippery egg in the other. After toying with the idea of shoving it in the ashtray, I wrestled with my two real options: I could continue to hold it for the rest of the drive or rid myself of it by eating it.[7]

11.

IT OFTEN FEELS LIKE I'm not so much living for the present as I am busy making memories for the future.

11 foods that don't have any calories

1.

BREATH MINTS (e.g., Tic Tacs, Altoids, Mentos).

2.

POPCORN AT THE movies (remarkably enough, this includes even the jumbo-size tub).[8]

3.

ANYTHING CONSUMED directly from the pot while standing over the stove.

4.

ANYTHING CONSUMED—whether a few nuts at a bar or a burrito the size of a marsupial—when you're drunk.

5.

CRUMBS.

6.

WHATEVER'S on your child's plate as you clean up.

7.

BIRTHDAY CAKE ON your birthday.

8.

SAMPLES—anything from muffin pieces at the Starbucks register to colossal wedges of brie at the grocery store.

9.

NOT THE FIRST, but the second and third bowls of cereal.

10.

THOSE THIN, AIRY breadsticks some restaurants place on the center of your table.

11.

ANY FOOD ITEM used as garnish.

11 thoughts about cars and driving

1.

I always get this weird sort of rush when an ambulance comes racing down the street, and I, along with all the other drivers, quickly pull over to let the more important vehicle pass. It's like all us little cars on the side of the road are cheering, "Go! Go! You can do it! Go, important ambulance, go!!!" The experience invariably leaves me feeling proud and giddy.

2.

WHEN I SEE SOMEONE sitting in a desired parking spot, and I mouth "are you leaving?" and they vehemently shake their head no, I take it personally and get upset.

3.

CAR HORNS should come with different options, different pitches, because one irritating beep doesn't cover the wide range of reasons we honk our horns. For example: there should be a gentle, bicycle bell–type honk that means, "Uh, you seem like a really nice person and I don't mean to bother you, but I just thought you should know that the light turned green."

4.

I JUST GOT REPULSED thinking about all the boogers that must be on the ground at stoplights.

5.

THIS IS ONE of those memories that out of nowhere resurfaces every now and then. I'm sixteen, taking Driver's Ed. The teacher asks which is safer: driving close to the other cars on the highway, or keeping your distance from them. I guessed the former, thinking there was safety in numbers. Of course this is totally wrong. At some point in my twenties I realized why this trivial memory was lodged so prominently in my brain: I had guessed "groups" because that was how the teen world operated, in cliques. It was only later, in college, that I discovered the fascinating, novel concept of individuality, of driving solo.

6.

I COULDN'T HAVE made this up: I saw a crossing guard finish up work, get into her car, blow through a red light, and crash into the side of another car.

7.

When a song that I can't stand comes on the radio in my car, or there seems to be an endless bombardment of commercials, I'll be exasperated at how unentertaining the station is, yet I'll keep listening. It's as if whatever station I turn on, I'm supposed to stick with it for the drive, this is my lot in life. And then it'll finally dawn on me: "Oh, yeah—I can change the station."

8.

SUCH PRETEEN, pre-reality contentment, being nine, in the front seat of the car with my dad, bringing McDonald's home for lunch, and the two of us sneaking hot, salty fries from the bag.

9.

PAY FOR THE PERSON behind you at the tollbooth; it invariably leaves the recipient feeling confused and suspicious, even though you were just doing it to be nice.

10.

PEOPLE WHO don't mouth "thank you" (or motion it by putting their hand up) after you let them into your lane, are terrible, evil people.

11.

WHEN I'M ON a road trip, and we approach the designated city after hours and hours of highway, I'll have mixed emotions. I'm excited to almost "be there" but I'm also sad about losing the kind of peaceful anonymity and uncomplicated remoteness that only huge, empty stretches of pavement can provide.

11 thoughts about pennies

1.

WHEN I COME ACROSS an old penny—recently I got one from 1952—there is a moment of excitement, like I have in my possession a treasure. It's something about this little piece of copper floating around for decades, it has seen the world, it is wise. I instinctively cast it aside for safekeeping, only to forget about it and/or spend it soon thereafter.

2.

I WAS WAY INTO my adult years before I really got the whole "leave a penny/take a penny" thing.

3.

IF I DROP a penny outside, I'll leave it, not because I don't like pennies, but because I'll think, "Well, there's a lucky penny for someone to pick up."

4.

CYNICISM = walking by a penny fountain and not making a wish.

5.

I JUST SCATTERED about fifty pennies outside on the sidewalk and stood back to see if anyone would pick them up. Just when I had a theory—that people seem to need money more than they need luck (only less well-off folks were picking them up)—a nicely dressed, wealthy-ish-looking woman proceeded to pick up a chain of seven pennies.

6.

Can you imagine how many unfunny penny jokes Penny Marshall and Penny Hardaway must have endured throughout their lives?

7.

I LOVE paying in pennies, and then how light and fresh my wallet feels after. It's cathartic in a way I don't fully understand.

8.

EVERY SO OFTEN I'll come across someone who mentions something about pennies being totally worthless, so worthless, in fact, that they even throw them out. That's sickening.

9.

I ONCE READ that if a penny was dropped from the top of a skyscraper, the force with which it landed could crush your skull. Living in a major city, this has haunted me for years. (Although there *is* something appropriate and poetic about being killed by a penny.) Is this true?

10.

THE IMAGE I EQUATE with the early 1900s—and I think I have *The Waltons* to blame for this—is of a rickety screen door slamming behind as a carefree someone saunters out of the general store holding an ice-cream cone, and the jolly owner, also satisfied with the transaction, is holding a penny.

11.

SEND ME your thoughts—about the proliferation of zines/the unpopularity of subtlety/elevator technology/this book/the genius of Albert Brooks/anything at all—and I'll send you a penny. ("Penny for your thoughts," c/o Andrews McMeel Publishing, 4520 Main Street, Kansas City, MO 64111. Please include a SASE.)

11 sub-languages of Americana

1.

HIGH SCHOOL YEARBOOK LANGUAGE

Stay cute!
2 cool 2 B 4gotten.
Have a great summer!

2.

MOVIE REVIEW LANGUAGE

"scintillating!"
"top notch!"
"a tour-de-force of ____ and _____ !"

3.

STARBUCKS LANGUAGE
tall
grande
mocha

4.

UBBY DUBBY LANGUAGE (origin: *Zoom*)
Tuboo bubad ubabubout huber nubew hubair cubut!

5.

OFFICE MEETING LANGUAGE
on the same page
push the envelope
a lot on my plate

6.

MAGAZINE COLLAGE CARD LANGUAGE

7.

RESTAURANT MENU LANGUAGE
20% gratuity will be added to parties of 6 of more
no substitutions
blue cheese: add 50¢

8.

MIXED TAPE TITLE LANGUAGE
Traveling Tunes
The Most Groovin' Songs Ever
The Best Tape Known to Man

9.

CHARADES LANGUAGE
first word
three syllables
sounds like

CEREAL BOX LANGUAGE

Good source of 11 essential vitamins and minerals
This product is sold by weight not volume. See side panel for details.
Serving suggestion

PRIME TIME LANGUAGE

Must see!
all new!
very special!

11 bad calls, bad people, and/or bad karma

1.

I WAS WALKING DOWN Michigan Avenue and I passed a guy asking for change. I had just moments before received a coupon for a free cup of coffee at Starbucks due to a mix-up with my order, and so I gave it to him. The man seemed pleased enough, and I continued on my way. Immediately, a well-dressed, executive-type woman tapped me on the shoulder. "Let me give you some advice, Sister," she whispered smugly. "When a bum's got better shoes than you, he probably doesn't need the money." And she walked away. I was left there feeling slighted. Not because I gave away the money (or coupon, in this case). No, I felt bad because, well, what's wrong with my shoes? I *like* my shoes.

2.

THE FOLLOWING occurred at a Chicago beef stand:

MR. BEEF GUY: Whadya want?

MY FRIEND PAT: I'll take a beef with hot peppers, and fries.

MR. BEEF GUY: You want a Coke with that?

MFP: No thanks. Just some water.

MR. BEEF GUY: Water? (PAUSES. LOOKS AROUND IN THAT TOUGH HARVEY KEITEL SORT OF WAY) You want water? Go down to the fuckin' lake!

3.

Dear Fine Person who Walked Away with Two of Our Brand New Flower Pots (you know, the ones that were meticulously hand-painted by a dear friend and were sitting right on our front steps)

I hate you.

Love,
Amy

4.

SOMETHING'S UP with my electromagnetic field: I've broken every computer I've ever owned. I seem to jam the Xerox machine every time I touch it. I go through Walkmans like paper towels.

5.

HONEST TO GOD, my dentist actually confessed that no, even he doesn't floss.

6.

WHEN I TOOK my four-year-old to see a Sunday matinee of *Space Jam*, the audience was, predictably, young kids and their parents. The preview? A montage of boobs, butts, and bad words from Rodney Dangerfield's latest movie.

7.

8.

MY FRIEND DEMA WATCHED A COP pull up behind a parked car and write a ticket for an expired meter. Then, instead of walking the six feet to the car, the cop decided to drive up alongside it. In doing so, he cut the corner too close and rammed into the car's left bumper, noticeably damaging it. The cop glanced around, leaned out his passenger side window, put the ticket on the car, and drove off.

9.

AND TO THE GUY driving down my street who saw me struggling to safely cross the street with three tiny humans and a Big Wheel, yet still decided you couldn't wait the extra ten seconds and flew through the intersection . . . thank you. You could have easily run us over, but instead you just blew exhaust in our faces. You're the man!

10.

THE HEALTH FOOD STORE in my neighborhood just closed down. In its place: Candy Junction. I'm all for junk food but this particular real estate 180 has some scary karma implications.

11.

I didn't get their names, but a <u>lot</u> of people littered.

11 unusual yet charming things about my friends

1.

AMY GETS sexually aroused when her boyfriend carries her groceries.

2.

WHEN NAKED, Charise tends to play the banjo.

3.

WHEN COOKING SOMETHING in his microwave, David never uses the handy preset increments (e.g., 20 or 30 seconds) but instead sets it for some odd amount of time (22 or 37 seconds) because it's more original, and because he can.

4.

JOHN wasn't allowed to use the word "very" growing up.

5.

How she managed to achieve this is beyond me, but Christine did not know what a spatula was until she was 16.

6.

DICK "OFFICIALLY" CHANGED his birthday from January 2 to May 2 because he couldn't stand having it the day after New Year's.

7.

JO REGULARLY COLORS in coloring books. She is sixty-one.

8.

EVEN IF there are three lanes on the highway that are for her desired direction, Renee insists on driving in the one lane directly under the sign, believing that it's more accurate.

9.

KIM, on the first day of freshman English, nonchalantly explained to the whole class that her bloodshot eyes were from a popped blood vessel, the result of pushing too hard when going to the bathroom.

10.

ANNE SERIOUSLY burned herself with corn chowder.

11.

LONG STORY, but the bottom line is, Laura once took a pregnancy test in the Vatican.

11 comparisons between the Church and the Mall— two modern places of worship

1.
Communion Wafers = Food Court

2.
Confessionals = Dressing Rooms

3.
Strive to Become a Better Person = Free Makeover

4.

Sermon = "Shoplifters Will Be Prosecuted"

5.

Closer to God = Escalators

6.

Lifelong Friends = Gift with Purchase of $40 or more

7.

Pray for Salvation = Pray for Parking

8.

Attend Every Weekend, Religiously = Attend Every Weekend, Religiously

9.

Greets You with Open Arms = Oversized
Disney Character Walking Around
Waving, Giving Hugs

10.

Bible to Help You Find Your Way =
Mall Directory
("YOU ARE HERE")

11.

Hallelujah! = Sale!

11 thoughts about sex

1.

AT INCREDIBLY crowded places—say a Bulls game or the airport—I can't help but look around in amazement: *every single person here* is the result of two people having sex.

2.

MY BROTHER found himself in a position where on one of the first dates with this one girlfriend, she said something which somehow evolved into a cutesy, inside joke between them. The only problem was, he wasn't paying attention when she initially said it, so he never really *got* the joke. He was, quite exactly, on the outside of their inside joke. She often referred to it and each time, he would muster up a lame smile or head-nodding chuckle. After so many months went by—they were pretty serious, together for over a year—there was just no way he could say, "You know what? I have absolutely *no* idea what this joke is about."

3.

I'VE SEEN IT: grown men exhibiting uncharacteristic patience and focus, all for the promise of maybe, if he tilts his head . . . *just* . . . *right*, glimpsing a sliver of breast on one of those scrambled sex channels.

RECENT NOCTURNAL celebrity conquests (in alphabetical order):

    Mikhail Baryshnikov

    Anthony Hopkins

    Kevin Spacey

    Ben Stiller

    Quentin Tarantino

Cameo! Please welcome Joe Krouse . . .[10]

5.

What does it mean if you fantasize about your mom having sex with Sigmund Freud?

6.

IT FEELS LIKE there should be some sort of formal, life-long bond you have with the person you lose your virginity to. Like that milestone-producing relationship, meaningful or not, warrants a special title. Years later, when you're married with kids and you run into this person, you know exactly how to address one another: "Oh, kids, I want you to meet Marc, my *Shtupper von Uno*."

7.

I DON'T THINK I could ever have sex with someone who used the phrase, "What a co-inki-dink!"

8.

RUNNER-UP for best Nude Dancer Sign of the year (spotted in South Beach, Florida):
LIVE, NUDE DANCERS!!! OPEN SIX PM TO SEX AM!!!

9.

IF PAGERS CAN VIBRATE, why not vibrators that page?
Damn. I swear my office pages me at the worst possible time.

10.

Really gorgeous, famous people who are
married to other really gorgeous, famous
people — do they ever get to the point
where when they're having sex they're
thinking, "What's that funny noise the
dishwasher's making?" and not, "Oh, my
God, I'm having sex with Demi Moore. I
can't believe it — Demi Moore !"

11.

MY FRIEND DAVID sat next to a nun on a recent plane ride.
They got to talking and he asked her what she missed most.
Without a second's thought, she replied, "Wearing blue jeans."

11 thoughts about food

1.

When a waiter says "good choice" after I order, I feel especially good, even proud. And when he says it to someone else, but not me, I feel as though I've failed some sort of restaurant pop quiz.

2.

PEOPLE HAVE THE STRANGEST reaction to free food when in an office environment. Casually announce that there's a platter of danish left over from some meeting, and the same coworkers who wouldn't get off the phone during a fire drill will come racing down the hall. "Free danish?! I must eat seven pieces of it right now, even though I just finished breakfast ten minutes ago." It's like the rules of calories and nutrition and acceptable eating habits in general do not apply when surrounded by staplers and cubicles.

3.

WHEN YOU'RE COOKING something as simple as, say, Minute Rice, do you have to keep looking back and forth at the directions twelve times?

4.

I WENT TO PAY for my tea and bagel at the local coffee-house and the woman behind the register said, "You know what? It's free today." "What? Why?!" I blurted out. "Just because," she replied. Wow. She intuitively senses I'm special, I thought. I bet I'm the only person she's ever given free tea to. She must be picking up on my unique energy; my significance; that I've been brooding and feeling contemplative lately; that I feel like I finally want to read Proust—*Proust!* How impressive! The other worker there tilted her head and whispered to me, "She does that all the time—to break up the monotony, you know?"

5.

I'VE KNOWN SOME PEOPLE—not many, but some— who occasionally will say, "Oh, I forgot to eat lunch today." *Forgot* to eat lunch? How does someone *forget* to eat? Forgetting the code to your cash machine card, or forgetting your best friend's birthday, I can understand. But forgetting an entire meal? No way.

6.

with J.
eating soup
(seafood bisque)
on the steps of the Guggenheim museum
Saturday 3:15 in the afternoon September 27, 1997

7.

THE OTHER DAY I was trying to throw out a bunch of
garbage while I was cooking dinner. I threw a handful of stuff
in the trash and everything went in except one little piece fell
on the floor. I bent down to pick it up to throw it out and realized it was the cap to the soy sauce, and I still needed that. I
thought it was really weird that it was the only thing that didn't
go in the can, like it missed on purpose or something.

8.

WHEN I GO OUT TO dinner, I'll work myself into a complete tizzy agonizing over everyone else's meals, thinking theirs looks so much better, and that I'd be much happier—not just with my dinner, but my life in general—if only I'd ordered what they did. In fact, I'll be overcome with food-doubt even when I'm thoroughly enjoying my dish. I think it would be helpful to start a standard restaurant policy where each person at the table automatically receives little side dishes of everyone else's meals, thus eliminating the whole Entrée Envy Syndrome entirely.

ANN KROUSE'S BEST **BBQ**UE RIBS EVER

3 slabs baby back ribs—extra lean
garlic salt
16 oz. jar of Open Pit Hickory Barbecue Sauce
16 oz. jar of Open Pit Regular Barbecue Sauce
16 oz. jar of honey

Preheat oven to 450°.

Place ribs on broiling pan and sprinkle both sides with garlic salt.

Bake ribs for 10 minutes to get rid of any excess fat. Drain fat.

Lower oven to 350° and bake for another 25 minutes.

Meanwhile, combine both barbecue sauces and honey in a pot and bring to a boil to thicken. Keep warm.

Turn oven to low broil. Baste ribs with the sauce; continue basting and turning every 10 minutes for another 20–30 minutes.

10.

I know a woman named Curry, another woman named Saffron, and a horse named Basil. I just think that's interesting.

11.

DON'T YOU LOVE how a waiter or waitress can be really unfriendly or even downright nasty throughout your entire meal, but then be all chipper as they hand you the bill adorned with a smiley face next to an emphatic "thank you" exclamation point! exclamation point! exclamation point! Like our memories are so short-term that we go, "Oh, look— a smiley face! I'm gonna tip EXTRA big!"

☺ Thank you !!!

11 things I'm curious about

1.

THERE WERE MEETINGS, people took notes, employees spoke solemnly, and everyone ultimately concluded that the ketchup label definitely needed the words "enjoy this with burgers and fries," and that consumers could not figure out on their own that certain products "make a great gift."

2.

How can we humans all have the same features — that is, a nose, a mouth, two eyes, two cheeks, etc. — yet, out of billions and billions, no two people look exactly alike? How does that work?

3.

IF A DOG breaks a mirror, does it get forty-nine years bad luck?

4.

WHY ARE NEWSLETTERS always so chirpy and unrealistically "up"? People who would never use an exclamation mark can't seem to get enough of them writing newsletters. ("We raised $250 at last month's Bowl 'N' Bake Sale—great job everyone!!!")

5.

What are the chances of meeting "Inspected by #9" at a party while wearing the garment they approved?

6.

WHEN WE WERE growing up, my dad slept with a baseball bat by his bed, as if he could save us from some sinister, armed evil by whacking them in the noggin Three Stooges–style.

7.

WHEN THOSE PEOPLE were writing the Bible, did they wake up Monday and go, "Shit, I gotta go to work," and pull the covers over their heads? Or did they jump out of bed every morning, energized by the realization that they were changing the world—or maybe they didn't sleep in the first place, too wired with the importance of what they were doing? While "at work," did they ever glance at their watches (sundials?) anxious for the arrival of 5:00? When they came home and their mates said, "How was your day? What did you do?" did they ever dare respond with "Fine" and "Nothing"?

8.

HOW COME YOU NEVER hear about a FedEx plane crashing?[11] It's like planes carrying packages and business documents are exempt from tragic destruction, but not humans.

9.

WOMEN DO THIS. I do this: reflexively offer up the price and location of a purchase in response to a compliment.
"I love that sweater!"
"Twenty bucks—Gap."

10.

WE KNOW who invented electricity . . . but what about the smaller yet also long-lasting discoveries: who was the first person to think to put butter on corn? First person to realize we have laps? First person to draw a star?

11.

I SAW a UPS truck driving through a cemetery.

11 olive stunts I would do for $5

1.

I WOULD eat an olive, slowly, very slowly, like, keep it in my mouth for six hours.

2.

I WOULD put a lot of keys in my pocket, stuff my shirt with ten or so cans of pitted olives, go to the airport, and when the metal detector went off and the security person thrusts that little dish in front of me, I would lift my shirt and let all the olives fall into it.

3.

I WOULD bump into someone drinking a martini and say, "You got martini on my olive!" And then switch voices pretending I'm them and say, "*You* got olive on my martini!"

4.

I WOULD go to get my hair cut, and when the woman asks me what kind of style I'm looking for, I'd ask her if I could look through a few of her hair magazines, and then when she came back I'd point to a picture of an olive.

5.

I WOULD, if ever asked to perform at Carnegie Hall, pay tribute to Andy Kaufman by concluding the show, not with milk and cookies as he did, but with milk and olives.

6.

I WOULD bring a wide range of olives—big, small, green, black, Greek—to one of those Sears portrait studios, and ask the guy to photograph this family of olives.

7.

I WOULD throw an olive at a stranger and when they got mad, I'd respond dramatically, "But olive you!"

8.

I WOULD picket in front of the grocery store shouting: "'Olive' backwards spells 'evil,' if you don't count the 'o'! 'Olive' backwards spells 'evil,' if you don't count the 'o'!"

9.

I WOULD go to this one Italian café by my house and order their large chopped salad (lettuce, chicken, pancetta, blue cheese, olives) and ask them if I could get it without the lettuce, chicken, pancetta, or blue cheese.

10.

I WOULD go to a used bookstore, buy *Remembrances of Things Past*, go to the part where Proust elaborates on the little madeleine cake, scratch out the word "madeleine" and write in "olive," and then put the book back on the shelf.

11.

I WOULD write a poem (rhyming) about olives, and send it to you, along with one complimentary olive. (Send $5 to Amy's Olive Poem, c/o Andrews McMeel Publishing, 4520 Main Street, Kansas City, MO 64111.)

11 thoughts about phones and answering machines

1.

I'VE HAD THIS ODD thing happen to me a number of times now where I've gotten to know someone pretty well through phone conversations. Then, when I actually meet the person, I am disappointed. Not because they are unattractive—because these people have actually turned out to be good-looking—but more because they turned out to be . . . human. I realized that when I spoke to them on the phone, I envisioned not really a distinct person with a face and body, but more like this vague, faceless *essence*, as if their whole personality manifested itself into an aura that wasn't exactly physical as we know it. So when I met these individuals, it was actually startling to see that they indeed had eyes and torsos and chins. Then later, when we'd be talking on the phone again, I realized I didn't picture them as they really looked upon our meeting, but rather they were back to that floaty-aura-thing they were for so long in my mind.

2.

ACTUAL MESSAGE FROM MY ANSWERING MACHINE!

AKR, it's DTJ, calling you back. Sorry I didn't get back to you jesterday [*sic*]. I was just thinking about calling you for no reason. I was thinking, "I should call Amy for absolutely no reason and say 'hi.'" And then *you* did. Cool. OK. I got big meetin's today, but give me a call—I'll be around. Uh, huh, it's true. OK. Bye.

3.

If you get arrested and you get to make your one phone call, and you get the person's answering machine — does that count?

4.

WHEN SOMEONE SAYS TO YOU on the phone, "Well, I'm going to let you go now," what they really mean is "Well, I'm bored now and/or I simply can't justify talking to you any longer."

5.

TALKING ON A CELL PHONE while pushing a stroller. I've seen it a few times now, and it is this one image out of all the others that assures me our society is fucked.

6.

MY SISTER BOUGHT an answering machine that (and I think this is a fair assumption) she believed to be new. But when she got it home and set it up, there were already messages blinking on it. The answering machine turned out to not be new at all; the messages were for the comedian Jackie Mason, who had been performing in town that past week.

7.

ISN'T IT ASTOUNDING how rapidly some people say their ten-digit phone number when leaving a message? Do they really believe the rest of the world is as familiar with their phone number as they are?

8.

I LIKE TO SAVE KIND, complimentary voice mail messages to play back again on those days I'm feeling especially loser-ish and defeated.

9.

SAYING "TAG, YOU'RE IT!" on someone's machine is like saying, "Hi! I like to say cliché, unoriginal things that were maybe funny once six years ago! Call me back!"

10.

There's always a moment of taboo weirdishness when you have to take a personal call in front of colleagues at work. Your voice shifts into whispery-embarrassed mode, and the overall mood in the room is that you are indeed some sort of freak for actually existing outside the office.

11.

I FEEL LIKE I'M ALWAYS waiting for that One Big Call, the call that's going to change my life in some fantastically profound way. What that call could possibly be, I don't know. An old boyfriend from seventh grade who's calling to say his life hasn't been the same ever since we broke up? A person with connections and power who likes my work and assures me that now, with his call, I have technically "made it"? Someone who never returned my phone call, but now offers some ego-pacifying and fairly plausible explanation as to why it's taken them two years to get back to me? In any event, there is an anxiety-filled, but not undelightful cloud of possibility looming in the air every time I come home to flashing new messages.

11 oddly touching photos

IT ALL STARTED WITH Michael Jordan. I met him last year (long story), and, apropos of nothing, he touched my big pregnant stomach for good luck. Knowing that the encounter could have profound significance on the life of my unborn child, and feeling that one can never really have too much good luck, I unleashed my belly on Chicago. For the last six weeks of my pregnancy, I waddled around the city with a camera, asking random people I encountered to touch my bloated stomach. The idea at first seemed silly and rather light: *Oh, won't it be fun to see how strangers react to such an odd request. Ha ha.* But people were surprisingly willing to pose with me (us). And it was nice, having someone I had just met touch someone I hadn't yet.

1.

Mac, a guy at
Urbus Orbis
coffeehouse

2.

Tom, the owner of
Urbus Orbis

3.

Jason from
MailBoxes, Etc.

4.

Ted, UPS driver

5.

Sahara, a checker at Target

6.

Karen, asst. manager at Baby Gap

7.

A taxi driver named Abraham

8.

The statue outside my office

9.

Ernie

10.

Leo, who developed my
film at Wolf Camera

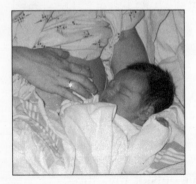

11.

Paris Anne

11 thoughts on the end

1.

IF I FOUND OUT that someone who I've seen recently just died, my immediate reaction isn't "Oh, how sad!" but rather, "But I just saw him!" As if death is more understandable when you haven't seen the person for a while.

2.

EVEN WHEN I'M HAPPY, and things are completely good, I'll be aware of this nagging "ugh" looming in the back of my mind. And then I'll pinpoint what it is: "Oh, yeah— I'm gonna die one day. This isn't forever." Basically, it's the college thing on a bigger scale: no matter how carefree and joyous and drunk you are, there's that little sober voice in the corner of your brain going, "Yeah, you laugh now, but you've still got that final in three weeks."

3.

I HAVE TO BE REMINDED—no, *convinced*—on a regular basis that death is not just some sort of unsubstantiated rumor. "Oh, my god, So-And-So just died. I can't believe it!" I require constant affirmation that humans really, truly die.

4.

WHEN SOMEONE DIES, I feel like the world should really stop, that we should be naked in the freezing cold and quit our jobs and suffer from their absence. That we should utter nothing for weeks but their name, over and over again until no other words make any sense. But the truth is, the person dies and minutes, maybe seconds later, we go out and grab a burger.

5.

SECONDS AFTER I RECEIVED a phone call that my parents' best friend died, my friend David bopped obliviously into my office, and started doing *Welcome Back Kotter* impersonations.

6.

I'M NOT 100 PERCENT SURE, but when I die, I think instead of a tombstone, I want to have a parking meter that reads "expired."

7.

I WONDER WHAT PERCENTAGE of people die with tampons in?

8.

I UNDERSTAND that manslaughter is a lesser crime than murder, but it seems like it should be the other way around. *Man. Slaughter.* It conjures up all sorts of large, sharp instruments. Murder, comparatively, at least sounds vague.

9.

IT'S SUCH AN ODD TERM, "the *late* so-and-so." But I guess it's true—you can't be any later than dead.
Is Ted coming to the party?
No, he's dead.
Oh, yes, he will be very late.

10.

WHEN I WAS A KID, someone told me that if you pressed directly on a certain spot—I believe it was somewhere around the neck—you would die instantly. They assured me it was extremely rare to die this way because the spot was hard to find. Despite the absurdity of this faux-medical advice, I have always carried the fear with me, that at any given time, my spot could accidentally be ignited by a hairdresser, a friend who hugged me too tight, a stumbling waiter.

11.

It's not death per se that freaks me out, but rather the permanence of it all.

11 endnotes

1.

Jeremy Solomon of First Books, Chicago.

2.

After an important conversation with the individuals I hoped would (and ultimately did) publish this book, I hung up the phone, and pulled down the little clock option on my computer. It flashed 11:11.

3.

The movie was *Strangers in Good Company*, directed by Cynthia Scott. It's sort of a chattier, girlier, more poignant *My Dinner with Andre*.

4.

These guys are really nice, really down to earth:
Tom Hanks, Michael Jordan.

5.

David Eggers is editor-at-large at *Esquire*, cofounded *Might*
magazine, cowrote *The Book of Cheese*, and, not surprising if
you know him, designs afghans.

6.

I left it.

7.

I ate it.

8.

Popcorn made at home, however, is caloric. And while on the subject of movie concessions: it's worth noting that the jumbo-size boxes of candy — when consumed at the movie — have exactly the same amount of calories as the small "normal" boxes you would buy elsewhere.

9.

About Charise. She is a Chicago-based artist and cartoonist. Her syndicated comic *Eye Spy* appears weekly in *New City* and *Miami New Times*. More important, she is tall and blonde.

10.

Joe Krouse is my brother. Joe says that there are two food groups: meat, and "no thanks." You'd really like Joe.

11.

After I wrote this, Charise phoned a couple days later to tell me her friend in San Francisco just lost a piece of original art because it was on a FedEx plane that crashed.